CONTENTS

WHAT'S MY IDEA?
	Page
Recording my Ideas	2
The Story Writing Form	4
Looking at Model Examples	6

DEVELOPING LANGUAGE
Adjectives, Adverbs and Verbs	10
Describing Colour	12
Ambitious Vocabulary	14
Figurative Language and Literary Devices	16
Creating Similes	18
Creating Metaphors	20
Creating Personification	22
The Personification of Abstract Nouns	24
Creating Hyperbole	26
Creating Oxymorons	27

DEVELOPING SKILLS
Sentence Structure	28
Sentence Openers	30
Senses	32
Show Don't Tell	34
Creating Fear and Suspense	36
Other Tips and Tricks	39
Punctuation	40
Writing Tasks	42

DEVELOPING STRUCTURE
Creating a Plan	48
Describing the Character	50
Describing the Setting and Weather	52
Creating your Character and Setting	56
Story Starter	58
First Paragraph	60
Developing the Main Story	62
Ending the Story	66

TASKS
Story Genres	69
Write a Story	70
Continue the Story	72
Write a Description	74
Write about an Experience	76
Write about a Picture	78

ASSESSING MY WORK
Checklist	80
Self-Assessment	81

NOTE FROM THE AUTHORS:

For most of us, just like real authors, coming up with the perfect story takes time and lots of practice.

This book offers a step-by-step guide to writing the perfect short story, by teaching children how to develop language, skills and structure.

We hope that you find it useful.

© 2019 Bright Light Education Ltd — Creative Writing Skills

WHAT'S MY IDEA?
Recording my Ideas

Before you start writing anything down, you need to come up with some great story ideas!

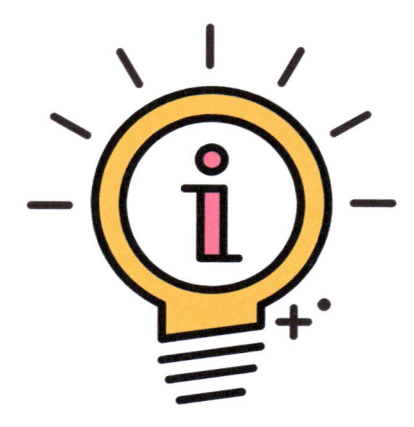

THERE ARE MANY WAYS TO DO THIS:

- Think about the storyline from novels that you have enjoyed.
- Think about other stories that your peers have written.
- Think about your own experiences. Could you turn them into a story?
- Ideally, you want a few interesting characters (not too many!) and a setting for the story to take place.
- Will your story start in the morning, afternoon or middle of the night?
- What time of year is it and what is the weather like?
- For the main part of the story, SOMETHING has to happen!
- Think about other stories you know and see if you can identify the main event or problem.

WHAT'S MY IDEA?

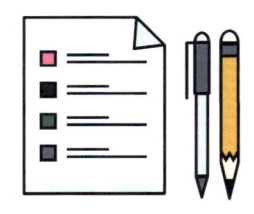

Use the following page to record different ideas - you never know when you might need them!

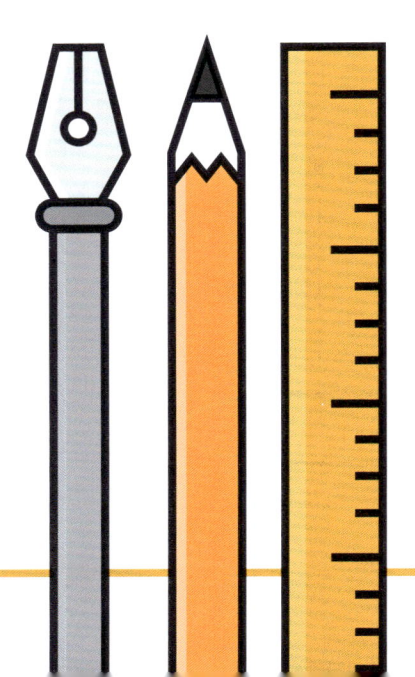

Creative Writing Skills

WHAT'S MY IDEA?

The Story Writing Formula

For some people, writing a story can be as easy as a walk in the park. For the rest of us, a few guidelines can be very helpful!

Remembering this formula can be a good starting point:

STORY =
LANGUAGE + SKILLS + STRUCTURE

This book explains how you can develop **language, skills and structure** in order to make your story as enticing as possible.

Perhaps think of story writing like baking a cake.

LANGUAGE

The **language** represents the icing on the top: this is pretty important so try to use a few good language features.

SKILLS

The **skills** are the sprinkles, the strawberries, the chocolate chips: you do not have to use them all, but they can help to turn your work (or cake!) into a masterpiece!

STRUCTURE

The **structure** represents the essential ingredients: the flour, butter, sugar and eggs. Without these, your story (or cake!) will not work.

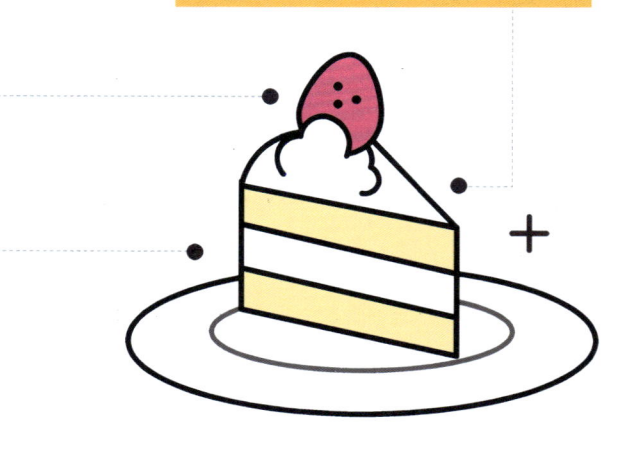

WHAT'S MY IDEA?

Let's look at this formula in greater detail:

LANGUAGE

Adjectives, Adverbs and Verbs

Ambitious Vocabulary

Figurative Language

SKILLS

Sentence Structure

Sentence Openers

Senses

Show Don't Tell

Fear and Suspense

The Power of Three

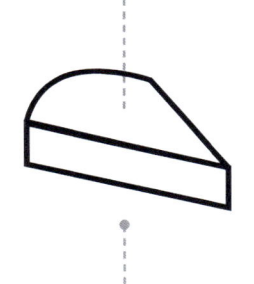

STRUCTURE

Story Starter
This is where you grab your reader's attention in the very first sentences. This may be as short as one sentence but no longer than four or five sentences.

First Paragraph
This is where your story begins. You are setting up the background to the story. You will probably introduce your characters and describe the setting, as well as having some action.

Middle Paragraphs
Within these paragraphs, you will continue the storyline, building up to your main event or problem. You should continue to include character and setting descriptions throughout.

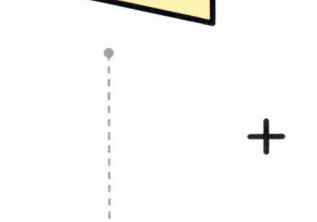

Final Paragraph:
This is where the main event or problem is resolved.

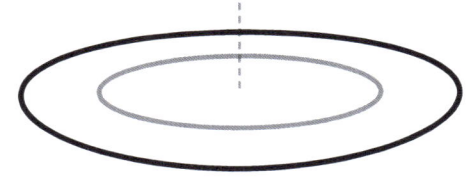

Story Ending:
Your final few sentences need to stand out and you must ensure that there is a clear ending.

WHAT'S MY IDEA?

Looking at Model Examples

Before you start writing, let's get some **inspiration** from other children's work!
Read over the beginning of the short story below and **highlight some of the words or phrases** that catch your attention.

The Haunted House

The wind screamed like a boiling kettle as it blustered around me. I'm not usually one who's frightened easily, but this unforgettable experience was striking terror in my heart.

Trembling with fear, I stumbled up to the house. Eerie chills, coming from the towering building, invaded me. The cobblestone pathways were violently cracked open by the jade green blades of grass. Audacious strands of ivy reached up into the unknown and clung desperately against the walls. The windows were latched shut as if the owner had a grudge against the outside, yet penetrating black smoke snaked slyly upwards, reaching the innocent cotton-ball like clouds and imprisoning them in their grasp.

An enormous wave of curiosity dragged me to the mahogany door standing proudly ahead. Taking a deep breath, I knocked. My heart pounded and every nerve in my body warned me to leave, but I was spellbound. No answer. Foolishly, I knocked again. This time, louder. Still no answer. Then, just as I was making the sane decision to leave, from the corner of my eye, I noticed a shadow forming from under the door. Petrified, cold sweat started to pour down my forehead. I froze and felt hypnotised as the door swung open.

Kai

WHAT'S MY IDEA?

Competition winners!

Here are story extracts from the winners of our 2020 Creative Writing Competition. We hope you enjoy reading them. **Highlight any words or phrases** that grab your attention.

Chloe
from category 1: Years 3 and 4 children

As climate change became even worse, soon there was going to be no hope left. The Arctic and Antarctic were melting, which meant cities were flooding. Even before the flooding, places like Australia were already gone, burnt and no life left. At the news headquarters in London, red warning lights rapidly flickered on and off. All of the screens said, "LONDON NOT SAFE". Splash! "What was that?" Everyone peered out of the shivering windows. "It's a massive wave!" People started to panic. "Follow me!" I shouted and I led the terrified workers out of the BBC tower. Breathing fast I tried to grasp my camera, but I was too late. The wave swallowed me. I squeezed my eyes shut, my soaked clothes weighing me down. Suddenly somebody caught my arm, and I was being pulled up to safety, on to a boat. I sat shivering as I watched the sight of my hometown drowning, sinking into the icy slush, as if it was being pulled down, like I was.

WHAT'S MY IDEA?

Anaiya
from category 2: Years 5 and 6 children

The first rays of morning sunlight caressed Emma's ashen face. Her limp, worn out body slid under the soft white coverlet as her clammy eyes sealed like shells. She began to ponder…

Emma's steady pace led her onto the escalators, down to the platform of the underground. Peering into the dark shadow distance, she could see the vivid headlights of the 11:20 train illuminating the pitch-black tunnel. WHOOOSH! HISSS! SCREEECH!

The train deafened Emma's ears as it came to an abrupt halt, bringing with it a hurricane of madness that tumbled her golden tresses across her face. There was only one thing she desperately wanted to do: scramble into the carriage of the train. Packed with a forest of passengers, Emma knew they would squash her, like a rolling pin flattening dough. With her heart throbbing like a rapid drum beating, she let out a squeal of delight and stepped inside.

As the train crawled away, she unzipped her leather rucksack, took out a red shiny apple and grazed on a mouth-watering bite. Emma felt comforted and the sweet taste was succulent. She closed her eyes for some time. There was a calm silence…

WHAT'S MY IDEA?

Amal
from category 3: Years 7 and 8 children

> Thunder rumbled. Grey dark clouds raged into war, dictating the sky and threatening to explode. Lightning awakened the river; transforming as the waves became huge and angry. The sky shed tears, pounding against the land. Buildings rose to the occasion donning their best grey suits. This was London.
>
> I stared out into the gloom; fists clenched. The rain thrashed against my head. The tall monument of Buckingham Palace towered above me, eerily. I, Henrietta Hardrada, the rightful Queen of England should be there, sitting on my throne, wrapped up in a snug blanket with a crown upon my head. But instead here I am in this cottage full of disasters. A leaky roof, cracked floorboards and ripped curtains surround me. Tonight, I will avenge my brother Harald's death and I will reclaim the crown.

CREATIVE WRITING COMPETITION

for West London children from ages 7-13

Our Creative Writing Competition takes place once a year and is for children in years 3-8. In 2020, the theme was "London" and we had 88 entries across **3 categories (years 3-4, years 5-6 and years 7-8).**

The aim of the competition is to encourage children to write creatively by coming up with their own 500 word short story. We hope it inspires children and engages them with writing!

DEVELOPING LANGUAGE

Let's start by learning how to develop language.

Adjectives, Adverbs and Verbs

The simplest way in which you can enhance your writing style is by adding in some **adjectives** and **adverbs,** and by changing your **verbs.**

Look at the following example:

'Enzo walked towards the castle.'

Let's add some **adjectives**

'Enzo walked towards **the towering medieval** castle.'

Now, let's add an **adverb**

'Enzo walked **anxiously** towards the towering medieval castle.'

Now let's change the **verb**

'Enzo **shuffled** anxiously towards the towering medieval castle.'

See if you can do the same! Use the collection of adjectives, adverbs and verbs on the following page to help you.

Marcus ate a pizza. _____

The cat slept on the sofa. _____

Tasha went to the cinema. _____

10 | Creative Writing Skills

DEVELOPING LANGUAGE

Here's a bank of adjectives, adverbs and verbs to get you thinking!

ADJECTIVES

Small - miniature
Big - colossal
Bad - atrocious
Good - marvellous
Quiet - inaudible
Loud - deafening
Fast - brisk
Slow - sluggish
Old - mature
Young - youthful
Hard - mind-boggling
Easy - straightforward

People:
- Adventurous
- Aggressive
- Clumsy
- Considerate
- Obnoxious
- Talented

Objects:
- Colourful
- Distinct
- Filthy
- Magnificent
- Old-fashioned

Positive Feelings:
- Comfortable
- Courageous
- Determined
- Elated
- Enthusiastic

Negative Feelings:
- Anxious
- Ashamed
- Bewildered
- Embarrassed

ADVERBS

Angrily
Anxiously
Cautiously
Cheerfully
Courageously
Elegantly
Enthusiastically
Foolishly
Frantically
Inquisitively
Nervously
Shyly

When:
- Afterwards
- Beforehand
- Early
- Recently
- Tomorrow
- Yesterday

How often?
- Always
- Constantly
- Occasionally
- Regularly
- Usually

Where?
- Above
- Below
- Downstairs
- Everywhere
- Wherever

How much?
- Almost
- Completely
- Entirely
- Totally

VERBS

Bounce
Crawl
Dash
Giggle
Sigh
Smirk
Sneak
Stumble
Tremble
Whisper
Yawn
Zoom

Thought:
Contemplated, daydreamed, pondered, reflected, wondered.

Said:
Announced, argued, babbled, confessed, denied, dictated, muttered, roared, snapped, squeaked.

Went:
Bounced, crawled, dashed, dawdled, hobbled, marched, prowled, scrambled, wandered.

Broke:
Burned, melted, smashed, snapped, shattered, cracked, fractured, ruptured, burst, split.

DEVELOPING LANGUAGE

Describing Colour

Colour is such a wonderful thing to be able to describe and, on occasion it is fine to use the generic terms of each colour. However, we think you can do better than this! Words to describe colour can express emotion and feeling within a story and bring it to life so start by thinking about *how* it is coloured.

Use the examples below to help you be more specific:

How is it coloured?

Ablaze with…	Beaming with…
Bold…	Bright…
Brilliant/vivid/intense/vibrant…	Dappled with…
Deep/dark/rich…	Delicate/subtle/slight…
Electric…	Festive…
Fiery…	Flamboyant…
Glistening/glittering/shining with…	Iridescent…
Tinged with…	Faded…
Light/pale…	Dotted with…
Muted tones of…	

Colour Compounds

Compound adjectives are made when you join two adjectives together, with a hyphen in between. When describing a noun with colours, make it come to life by turning it into a compound adjective.

For example: His eyes were pistachio-green.

Colour Metaphors

It's easy to use metaphors when describing the colour of something. Think of an object that is the colour you want to describe and use that word alone.

For example: Its eyes were fire, glistening in the dark.

This suggests that the eyes are orange-yellow in colour.

For example: Golden fields lined the horizon.

This implies the fields were a glistening yellow.

Crimson	**Ruby**
Cherry	**Scarlet**
Tangerine	**Fiery**
Marmalade	**Pumpkin**
Canary	**Mustard**
Dandelion	**Amber**
Emerald	**Olive**
Moss	**Mint**
Cobalt	**Teal**
Cerulean	**Azure**
Sapphire	**Navy**
Oxford Blue	**Royal Blue**
Lavender	**Grape**
Aubergine	**Amethyst**
Fuchsia	**Magenta**
Bubble-gum	**Blush**
Mahogany	**Tan**
Cinnamon	**Coffee**
Charcoal	**Ebony**
Midnight	**Midnight**
Graphite	Slate
Pewter	Smoke

CREATIVE WRITING SKILLS © 2019 Bright Light Education Ltd

DEVELOPING LANGUAGE

Colour Similes

Similes work well with colours too. Again, compare the colour of something with another object. This time, use *like* or *as* to compare the two.

For example: The snake's skin was like a wrinkled olive.

This not only gives us detail about the texture of the snake's skin, but also suggests it was a murky-green colour.

Activity 1:

Look at the colours down the centre of the page. Can you think of your own words to describe these colours?

Activity 2:

See if you can describe the image below, using a range of colour description!

For example:

Ahead of me stood fields ablaze with egg-yolk yellow rapeseed. Glancing upwards, the piercing cerulean sky stretched out as far as the eye could see.

Your turn:

© 2019 Bright Light Education Ltd — Creative Writing Skills | 13

DEVELOPING LANGUAGE

Ambitious Vocabulary

It is important that you try to broaden your **vocabulary.** Using advanced and ambitious vocabulary will help to embellish your story, accentuate meaning and enthral your reader.

TOP TIP!

- Teach yourself a new word every day. Discover new words from books that you have read, vocabulary websites, apps, flashcards and vocabulary books. There are lots of resources out there to help you to learn new words!

- Read. Reading a wide range of books will naturally help to boost your vocabulary.

- Talk to your family about the new words that you have learned and what they mean. Practise using the word in a sentence.

- Make your own flashcards with the word on one side and the definition/ example sentence on the other side. By making them yourself, you are more likely to remember them.

Use the vocabulary on the following page to fill in the gaps.

1. Be careful! He is in a rather _____ mood and could attack you at any moment.

2. The doctor was _____ that the patient should take the medication quickly.

3. The company is _____ for not paying its bills on time.

4. I loved my _____ trek to the summit.

5. Even though Meera was younger than the other children in the competition, her _____ attitude meant that she never gave up.

14 | Creative Writing Skills © 2019 Bright Light Education Ltd

DEVELOPING LANGUAGE

Here is a list of ambitious vocabulary.

See if you can find out what each word means and then write it in your own sentence.

WORD	SENTENCE
Absent-minded	
Adamant	
Amiable	
Arduous	
Audacious	
Belligerent	
Cantankerous	
Competent	
Deceptive	
Effortless	
Exhilarating	
Facetious	
Fiendishly	
Intolerant	
Ludicrous	
Monotonous	
Notorious	
Onerous	
Opulent	
Perplexed	
Placid	
Prosperous	
Spontaneous	
Sporadic	
Tenacious	
Tenuous	
Vivacious	

DEVELOPING LANGUAGE

Figurative Language and Literary Devices

Using **figurative language** and **literary devices** in your writing can really help to make your story unique. Figurative language is great because it helps to create an image in the reader's mind. Create your own phrases using your imagination! Try to remember figurative language by using the acronym, **SHAMPOOP!**

S — SIMILE
A descriptive phrase that compares two things by using 'as…as' or 'like'.

For example: He was as proud as a peacock.

H — HYPERBOLE
An exaggerated statement.

For example: I'm so hungry I could eat a horse.

A — ALLITERATION
A repeated letter or sound at the beginning of several words.

For example: The hungry hippo.

M — METAPHOR
A descriptive phrase that compares two things, by saying that one thing IS another thing.

For example: The snow is a white blanket.

P — PERSONIFICATION
Making something do the action of a human or have the feelings of a human.

For example: The rain wept.

O — ONOMATOPOEIA
Using words that sound like the thing they are describing.

For example: Bang! Crash!

O — OXYMORON
A phrase that includes words which seem to contradict each other.

For example: A deafening silence.

P — PATHETIC FALLACY
Connecting human emotions/moods with objects of nature.

For example: The sombre clouds darkened our mood.

---

16 | Creative Writing Skills © 2019 Bright Light Education Ltd

DEVELOPING LANGUAGE

Read the following paragraph and, using a key, underline in different colours all the different forms of figurative language that you can spot.

"Dinner time?" Sherry enquired, jumping up from the sofa like a piece of toast from the toaster. She had not eaten all day and was ravenous. "Hurry up! I am so hungry I could eat a horse!".

Sherry's mother placed the dinner on the table. Sizzling sausages and milky mash, her favourite. Sherry's eyes widened as she plunged her fork into the juicy sausages, which were begging to be eaten. Devouring every mouthful, Sherry demanded more.

"Your stomach is a bottomless pit!" Sherry's mother exclaimed.

"Milkshake!" Sherry squealed, as she grabbed her ice-cold glass filled to the brim with frothy, creamy milk and blended bananas. Slurp! Slurp! Slurp!

After a few minutes, everything on the table was gone. Sherry had demolished her dinner and was ready to return to the sofa.

Colour: Figurative language:
- ☐ - **Simile**
- ☐ - **Hyperbole**
- ☐ - **Alliteration**
- ☐ - **Metaphor**
- ☐ - **Personification**
- ☐ - **Onomatopoeia**

DEVELOPING LANGUAGE

Creating SIMILES

Similes can create wonderful images in readers' minds allowing them to visualise the comparison. However, you've got to try and bring them to life. Let's have a go and look more closely at **similes.**

Big	As big as an elephant	**Innocent**	As innocent as a lamb
Small	As small as the point of a needle	**Playful**	As playful as a kitten
Fast	Like a rocket	**Crazy**	As nutty as a fruitcake
Slow	Like a snail	**Angelic**	Like an angel
Brave	As brave as a lion	**Lazy**	As lazy as a sloth
Cunning	As cunning as a fox	**Loud**	Like a screaming baby
Dark	As black as coal	**Angry**	Like a volcano
White	As white as a dove	**Quiet**	Like a pin dropping
Blind	As blind as a bat	**Light**	As light as a feather
Flat	As flat as a pancake		

When writing **similes,** try not to use all the obvious ones that everyone uses!

Step 1: Think of the adjective you want to make a comparison about.

Step 2: Brainstorm all the ways in which you could describe that adjective.

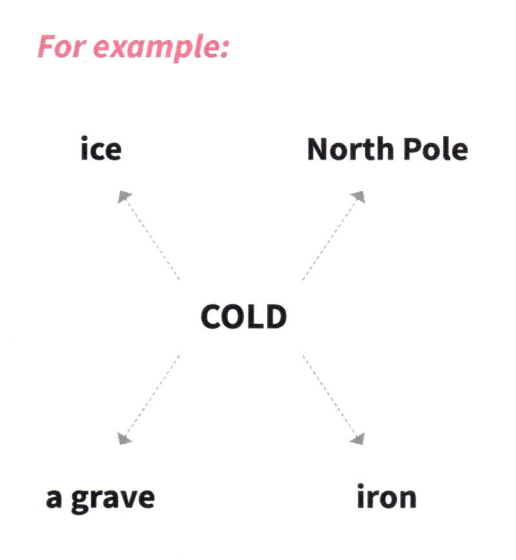

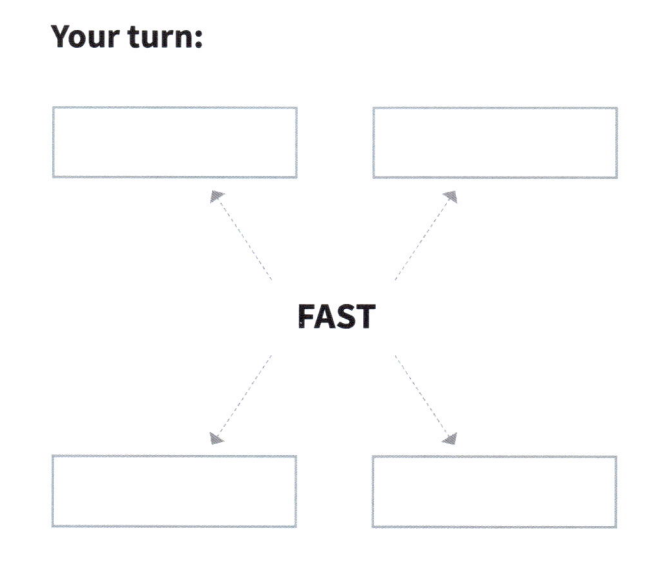

For example:

ice   North Pole

COLD

a grave   iron

Your turn:

☐   ☐

FAST

☐   ☐

DEVELOPING LANGUAGE

The next step is to try to make them even more unique, so that they stand out. Read the example below and then try to write your own examples.

Mia ran as fast as a cheetah.

Let's add an **adjective** before the final noun.

*Mia ran as fast as a **racing** cheetah.*

Now, let's add an **extra clause after the simile**

*Mia ran as fast as a racing cheetah, **that's spotted her prey in the distance.***

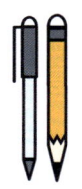

Your turn:

My nephew is as cunning as a fox.

Let's add an **adjective** before the final noun.

My nephew is _____

Now, let's add an **extra clause after the simile.**

My nephew is _____

Your turn:

Jess was as slow as a snail.

Let's add an **adjective** before the final noun.

Jess was _____

Now, let's add an **extra clause after the simile.**

Jess was _____

DEVELOPING LANGUAGE
Creating METAPHORS

Metaphors are similar to similes. They compare two things. However, rather than using 'as…as' or 'like', a metaphor says that one thing IS another.

Some people struggle to create metaphors, so why don't you create a simile first, and then remove the 'as … as' or 'like'?

'The snow was like a white blanket.'

'The snow was a white blanket.'

'The classroom was like a zoo.'

'The classroom was a zoo.'

Here is a list of some metaphors:

The hospital was a refrigerator.

Their home was a prison.

His heart is a cold iron.

Her long hair was a flowing golden river.

The computers at school are old dinosaurs.

The falling snowflakes are dancers.

The wind was an angry witch.

Her angry words were bullets to him.

Your brain is a computer.

I am so excited. My pulse is a race car.

The moon is a white balloon.

The stormy ocean was a raging bull.

Her spidery hand wrapped around the boy's wrist.

His crocodile jaws snapped shut.

The lesson was a recipe for disaster.

DEVELOPING LANGUAGE

Let's have a go at creating metaphors.

Activity 1:

See whether you can finish these sentences by adding a metaphor. If you are stuck, remember to think of a simile first and then turn it into a metaphor!

When she laughed, she was _____

The waves hitting the beach were _____

At the party, Mariam was _____

As he stepped inside, the room was _____

The trees in the storm were _____

Activity 2:

Another fun activity is to try to describe yourself using only metaphors!

For example:
I am a tornado.
My hair is a large bowl of spaghetti.
My laugh is a bubbling bottle of champagne.

Your turn!

_____
_____
_____

Activity 3:

Can you create your own metaphors for the following nouns:

The sun: _____

The trees: _____

A castle: _____

DEVELOPING LANGUAGE

Creating PERSONIFICATION

We love **personification!** To create personification, simply give your object a human action or feeling.

Here is a list of examples of personification:

The moon **smiled.**

The tower **felt proud** as the children climbed it.

The wind **wrapped itself** around my face.

The ocean waves **swallowed** the boat.

The alarm clock **screamed** at me this morning.

Lightning **danced** across the sky.

The wind **howled** in the night.

The old chair **moaned** when the boy jumped on it.

The moon **played hide and seek** with the clouds.

My flowers were **begging** for water.

The ivy **wove its fingers** around the fence.

Look at the image. How could you describe the scene, using personification?

DEVELOPING LANGUAGE

To help you come up with **personification,** look at the outline of the person below. Around the person, write down all the things that humans can do and all the different feelings that humans can have. Some examples have been given to start you off.

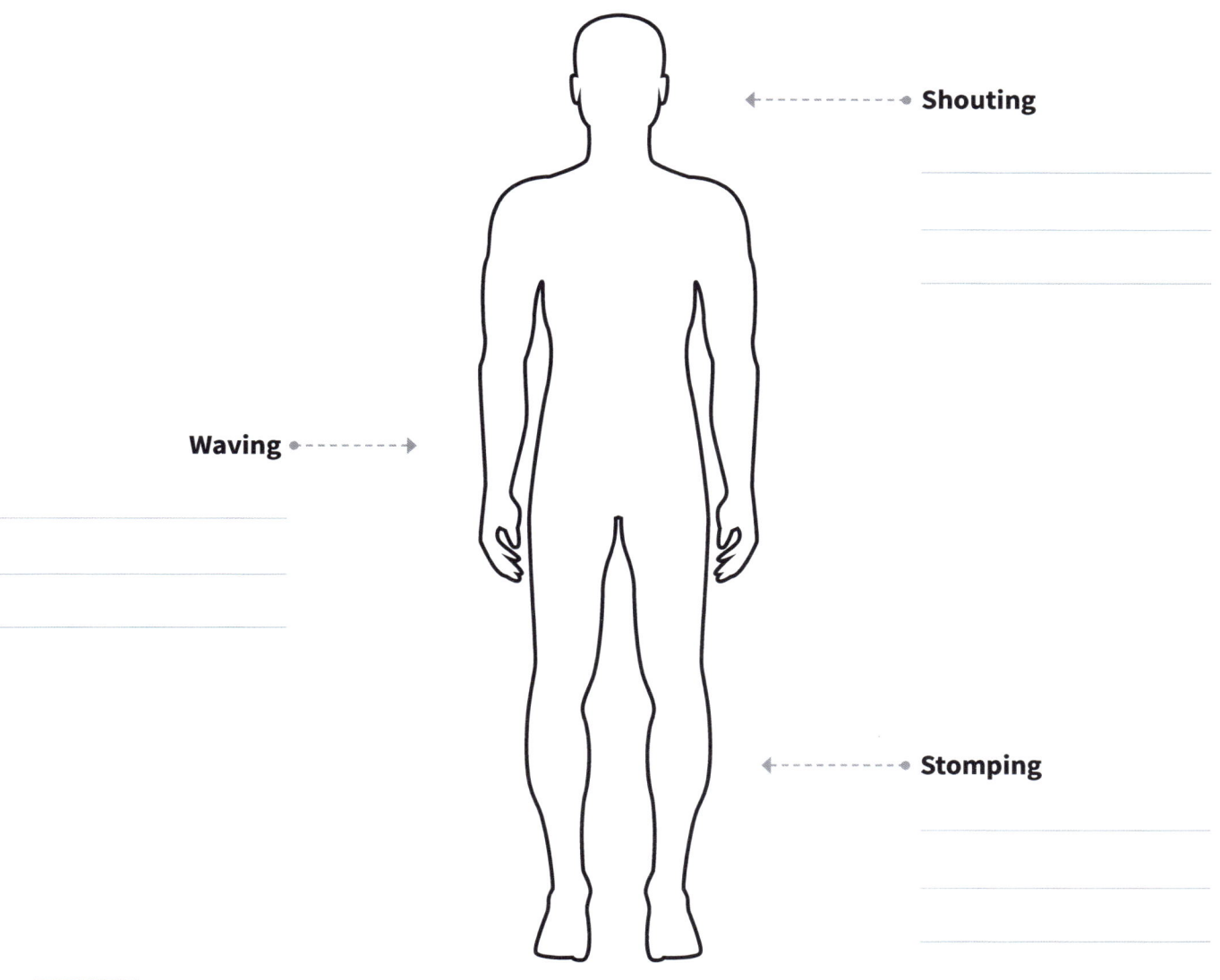

Shouting

Waving

Stomping

Using these human actions and feelings, try to create your own examples of personification for:

The car: _____

The door: _____

The leaves: _____

DEVELOPING LANGUAGE

The Personification of Abstract Nouns

Personification can also be an effective and powerful way to describe abstract nouns, **especially emotions like love or anger.**

STEP 1:

Look at the list below, separated into positive and negative emotions.

Positive emotions	Negative emotions
Beauty	Anger
Bravery	Confusion
Calmness	Envy
Courage	Fear
Happiness	Grief
Honesty	Hatred
Hope	Horror
Joy	Hunger
Love	Sadness
Luck	Sorrow

DEVELOPING LANGUAGE

STEP 2:

If you are writing a sentence using a positive abstract noun, think of a person who brings you happiness and describe their actions towards you:

For example:

Cuddles me, comforts me, holds my hand, hugs me, wraps its arms around me.

If you are writing a sentence using a negative abstract noun, think of a monster and describe their actions towards you!

For example:

Rips me apart, steals my heart, leaves me helpless, eats away at me, cripples me, attacks me.

STEP 3:

Now personify your abstract noun to create a powerful sentence about your character.

For example:

Happiness wrapped its arms around me.

Sadness tore me open and left me helpless.

Your turn!

Try to finish these sentences:

Courage _____

Love _____

Anger _____

Fear _____

DEVELOPING LANGUAGE

Creating Hyperbole

Hyperbole is the trick of exaggerating a situation, action or feeling by using extreme language. It intensifies the image created in the reader's mind and it has to be something which is not actually possible. It is also often used for humorous effect.

Some common everyday hyperbole:

- *I've told you to do your homework a million times today!*
- *Our teacher gave us a tonne of homework.*
- *It's so cold even the polar bears are wearing gloves!*
- *I'm so hungry, I could eat a horse!*
- *Her brain is the size of a pea.*
- *I have a million things to do today.*
- *She could smell it a mile away!*

It can be hard to use hyperbole in your writing so use these simple steps to help:

1. Think about anything you want to describe.
2. Now, think about a particular quality of that thing. **For example:** Its size or beauty.
3. Finally, get those creative juices flowing and exaggerate!

For example:

The play was very long.

Now add some exaggeration: The play was going on forever.

Now make it even more exaggerated and amusing: The play was going on for as long as it took to build the Great Wall of China.

Activity: Create your own hyperbole from the topics below. Try not to create a simile!

Something heavy. _____

Something spicy. _____

Being very tired. _____

DEVELOPING LANGUAGE

Creating Oxymorons

An **oxymoron** is a figure of speech that uses contradictory terms. The most common form of oxymoron involves an oxymoron-noun combination of two words.

Some examples:

- Act naturally
- Alone together
- Amazingly awful
- Bittersweet
- Clearly confused
- Dark light
- Deafening silence

- Definitely maybe
- Farewell reception
- Growing smaller
- Jumbo shrimp
- Only choice
- Open secret
- Original copy

- Painfully beautiful
- Passive aggressive
- Random order
- Small crowd
- Sweet sorrow
- True myth
- Walking dead

It can be hard to use oxymorons in your writing so use these simple steps to help:

1. Think of characteristics of a description for something.

    For example: Buying Christmas presents.

    First characteristic: *Buying presents can be a painful task of visiting the shops amongst the crowds, and trying desperately to find that perfect present in time.*

    Second characteristic: *Buying presents can lead to huge excitement that Christmas is near, and this time of year brings joy and happiness to many.*

2. In order to create an oxymoronic statement, combine the two characteristics:

    Buying Christmas presents fills me with a painful pleasure.

    In the above sentence, *"painful pleasure"* is a contradictory phrase, but its meaning makes sense in light of buying Christmas presents' contradictory but complementary effects.

    Activity 1:
    Have a go at writing some sentences using the oxymorons above.

    _____
    _____

    Activity 2:
    Now have a go at creating your own oxymorons!

    _____
    _____

DEVELOPING SKILLS

This chapter teaches you how to develop skills.

Sentence Structure

To begin with, try to vary the **structure** of your **sentences.**

1) USE SHORT SIMPLE SENTENCES.

Sometimes you can create a dramatic effect by writing short, snappy sentences.

For example: The boy froze. He twitched.

2) USE LONG SENTENCES SEPARATED BY COMMAS.

Create a never-ending, continuous feeling by using a long sentence. Create a long sentence when you really want the reader to picture something or someone in their minds.

For example: Toys lay strewn across the floor, tissues littered the couch, scraps of food from previous meals were encrusted into the gaps between the floor boards while the dust gathered on every visible surface.

3) CREATE A COMPOUND SENTENCE.

Use two main clauses and a co-ordinating conjunction to create a compound sentence. The acronym, FANBOYS, can help you (For, And, Nor, But, Or, Yet, So).

For example: Izzy can be energetic, but she can also be hard-working.

4) CREATE A COMPLEX SENTENCE.

Use a main and subordinating clause with a subordinating conjunction to create a complex sentence. Embedded clauses also help to create complex sentences. The acronym, ISAWAWABUB can help you (If, Since, As, When, Although, While, After, Before, Until, Because).

For example: You need to work hard if you want to become a doctor.
For example: The man, who was unusually tall for his age, struggled to find shoes that would fit him.

5) INCLUDE A RHETORICAL QUESTION.

Rhetorical questions can help to share the emotions of the character or can build suspense in your story.

For example: What was I supposed to do now?

DEVELOPING SKILLS

Let's have a go at changing the structure of your sentences.

Using the sentences below, see whether you can re-write them in different ways. Can you change the 'feel' of the sentence just by changing the sentence structure?

For example: *The girl ate her lunch.*

Sentence Structure	Write your sentence!
Short Sentence	
Long Sentence	
Compound Sentence	
Complex Sentence	
Rhetorical Question	

For example: *The boy stood in front of the house.*

Sentence Structure	Write your sentence!
Short Sentence	
Long Sentence	
Compound Sentence	
Complex Sentence	
Rhetorical Question	

DEVELOPING SKILLS

Sentence Openers

When writing a story, you must remember to vary your **sentence openers.** Many of these are also Fronted Adverbials. Try to remember to vary your sentence openers by using the acronym, **ISPACED!**

I — -ing Word

Glancing across the room, Sylvie realised that something was missing.
For example: Entering, Clutching, Running, Hiding.

S — Simile

As quiet **as** a church mouse, Ishmael crept into his bedroom, so as not to wake his parents.
For example: As quiet as, As slowly as, Like a lion, Like a feather.

P — Preposition

Behind the sofa lurked some unwanted surprises.
For example: On, Under, Below, Beneath.

A — Adverb

Jauntily, the dog sloshed through the pouring rain.
For example: Foolishly, Shyly, Cautiously, Angrily.

C — Connective

When Charlotte stepped out of the house, she knew that winter had arrived.
For example: Although, Whenever, Finally, Since.

E — -ed Word

Mesmerised by the beauty of the lake, Jasmine thought back to why she had come here.
For example: Exhausted, Terrified, Shocked, Excited.

D — Dialogue

"Stop!" cried the young boy, moments before the train passed.

DEVELOPING SKILLS

Can you change the meaning of this sentence, by using different sentence openers?

For example: Aiden walked into the room.

Write your sentence!

I -

S -

P -

A -

C -

E -

D -

DEVELOPING SKILLS

Senses

Thinking about your **senses** is a brilliant way to come up with descriptive sentences. When you're writing, try to **PAUSE** and ask yourself the following questions:

What can my character
- **SEE?**
- **SMELL?**
- **TASTE?**
- **HEAR?**
- **TOUCH?**

Read the following paragraph and, using a key, underline in different colours all the different senses that you can spot!

I walked inside. Instantly, the sweet scent of the pink candyfloss begged me to come closer. The candyfloss looked like fluffy clouds balancing carefully on a stick. My taste buds tingled at the sight of the giant multi-coloured lollipops. Their shiny coating reminded me of a magical shell that I once found in the sea. The chocolate fountain was a dark flowing river and I was desperate to jump in and bathe. Clasping my marshmallow stick tightly, I slowly placed it into the smooth flowing fountain and turned it around until the pure white marshmallow had turned a rich deep brown. The taste was divine; the marshmallow melted on my tongue and the satisfying smell of cocoa comforted my soul. After devouring my delicious delight, I suddenly heard the sound of crackling popcorn from the corner of the room.

Colour: Sense:
- ☐ - **Sight**
- ☐ - **Smell**
- ☐ - **Taste**
- ☐ - **Sound**
- ☐ - **Touch**

DEVELOPING SKILLS

It's time to practise using your **senses.** The easy way to ensure that you include senses in your writing would be to write sentences like, "He could hear… He could smell… He could taste…". However, this is not particularly creative. Instead, try to avoid using the modal verb 'could' and go straight into the description. *For example:* 'A shrill-like noise pierced his ears' or, 'The pungent smell of rotting bins filled the air'.

Have a look at the word bank below to give you some other ideas for describing senses.

SMELL	SOUND	TASTE	TOUCH	SIGHT
Acrid	Bark	Acidic	Abrasive	Angular
Aromatic	Bellow	Appetising	Bumpy	Blushing
Fishy	Blare	Bitter	Bushy	Distinct
Foul	Cheep	Bland	Damp	Filthy
Fragrant	Chime	Creamy	Feathery	Gleaming
Fresh	Chirp	Full-Bodied	Frosty	Glowing
Minty	Chuckle	Flavoursome	Knobbly	Grotesque
Musty	Clash	Foul	Limp	Large
Nauseating	Crunch	Fruity	Moist	Long
Noxious	Howl	Peppery	Prickly	Murky
Odorous	Moan	Spicy	Rough	Rotund
Rancid	Pierce	Sugary	Slimy	Spotty
Pungent	Rumble	Succulent	Smooth	Stripy
Sharp	Sizzle	Tangy	Sticky	Thick
Sweet	Slurp	Zesty	Velvety	Translucent

See if you can describe the image below, focusing on senses.

DEVELOPING SKILLS
Show Don't Tell

Describing your characters' feelings is key to writing a good story. The reader wants to be able to put themselves in the shoes of your character, and the only way they can do this is if they know how your character is feeling. However, rather than simply stating the feelings, *show* the reader how your character is feeling, using the **Show Don't Tell** technique.

Describing emotions:

Noah felt scared. ⟶ Noah's stomach went scrambling up into his throat.

Alia was excited. ⟶ Alia's pulse started racing. Her eyes twinkled, and she let out a squeal of delight.

Describing emotions using dialogue:

"Do you want to go ahead?" Joe whispered nervously. ⟶ "Do you want to go ahead?" Joe whispered, his eyes darting from side to side.

Describing actions:

He cycled quickly. ⟶ His feet were pedalling furiously; his face was set in a mask of determination and houses zoomed past on either side.

Describing the noun:

The cat stared at me. ⟶ With glowing red eyes and a mouth of sharp teeth that emitted a yowl like a tiger, I knew that this small animal was dangerous.

Describing the setting:

It was a cold winter's day. ⟶ I lifted my head into the fierce, icy wind. Shivering, I wrapped my scarf tightly around my cold neck.

DEVELOPING SKILLS

It's time to practise the Show Don't Tell technique for describing **emotions.**

Complete the grid by thinking about all the different ways in which your body responds to these emotions. Create a bank of sentences for you to use in the future. Don't forget to use your senses to help you!

COLOUR - does part of your body change colour?

EYES - what do your eyes do?

HEART - what does your heart do?

MOVEMENT - does part of your body move? How?

NOISES - what noises does your body make?

SKIN - how does your skin react?

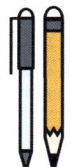

ANGRY	
EMBARRASSED	
EXCITED	
HUNGRY	*My stomach rumbled like thunder.*
NERVOUS	*The man was fidgeting and biting his nails.*
SAD	
SCARED	
SHOCKED	
TIRED	

DEVELOPING SKILLS

Creating Fear and Suspense

To make your story captivating, you will probably want to include some **fear or suspense.** Here are some ways in which you could create these emotions. Many of these skills build on from what you have learned already.

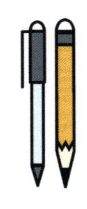

1. Show Don't Tell

Use Show Don't Tell but extend your sentence with an adjective, adverb or simile!

For example:

Daisy was nervous = Millions of tiny goose bumps jumped out from Daisy's arm, like oil from a sizzling frying pan.

Your turn!

Reuben was terrified = _____

2. The Personification of Abstract Nouns

Only when your story is reaching a climax, you may like to use personification to describe an extreme emotion.

For example:

Fear strangled him and left him gasping for air.

Your turn!

Fear…… _____

3. Senses

Use all your senses to really help the reader to immerse themselves in the story.

Can you highlight the senses used in these three sentences?

I heard a peculiar rustling sound in the undergrowth and caught a glimpse of something moving away behind the trees. Suddenly the ground began to tremble. I spun around and gasped.

4. Panic Conjunctions

Try not to use 'suddenly' more than once in a story!
Consider using some of these other panic connectives:

For example:

Abruptly, all at once, all of a sudden, a moment later, just then, quickly, unexpectedly, without warning.

5. Repetition

Try repeating a word, either with consecutive words, or at different points in the paragraph or sentence.

For example:

Tap. Tap. Tap.

6. Onomatopoeia

There are lots of great onomatopoeic words for creating suspense, but here are some of our favourites:

For example:
Crash, creek, crunch, grumble, growl, howl, moan, pitter patter, rattle, scream, screech, shriek, smash, thud.

Can you think of any more spooky onomatopoeia? _____

7. Pathetic Fallacy

Don't forget to consider what the weather would be like at certain stages in the story. What atmosphere do you want to create? Does the weather change at the climax of the story?

For example:
The thunder rumbled in the distance.

What atmosphere does this create? _____

8. Short Sentences

Use short sentences to keep the reader on the edge of their seat!

For example:
She froze. She panicked. She gasped.

DEVELOPING SKILLS

9. Rhetorical Questions

Use a rhetorical question to share the thoughts of your character.

For example:
Where am I? How will I get out of here?

10. Tricolon

Tricolon is a literary term for a series of three words, phrases or clauses, which come in quick succession next to each other. Tricolons are used when you want to emphasize your point more powerfully.

For example:
A gust of ghostly wind almost swept Julian off his feet. Silence. Scream. Panic.

11. The Three Bad Dash Question

Linked to the idea of tricolons, the Three Bad Dash Question helps to enhance a negative feeling, by using three bad adjectives. You then use a dash and a question to add suspense.

For example:
Greed, hatred, jealousy - which of these was Jacob's worst attribute?
Exhaustion, heatstroke, thirst - which would kill her first?

Activity:
Have a read of the short example below. Can you highlight which techniques the author has used to create suspense?

There's nothing to worry about, she told herself as she started to walk nervously down the stairs. It's just a storm coming. Tap. What was that noise? Glancing towards the window, she noticed the tree outside tapping on the glass. Relieved, she continued to walk down the stairs. Tap. Her heart began to beat faster as she held onto the banister with a tight grip. Tap. There it was again. This time, it was coming from the downstairs kitchen.

Other Tips and Tricks

Here are a few more tips and tricks that you could include in your writing!

1) Try zooming in.
Start with the big picture and then zoom in.
For example: On a large green hill, there was a forest. In the forest, there was a small house. In that house lived Mr and Mrs Garcia and their three children.

2) Use negative description.
Try describing what was not there.
For example: Abdul went to the park but there was no slide, no children, no fun.

3) Try foreshadowing.
Try foreshadowing or guessing ahead to what's going to happen later in the story.
For example: I knew it would be a bad day when the alarm didn't go off and there was nothing to eat for breakfast.

4) Try changing the word.
Try changing how a word is written to show its meaning.
For example: Emily crept towards the door. CRRRRAAAASSSSHHH!

5) Include a stream of consciousness.
Try using a rhetorical question to show what the character is thinking.
For example: What was I supposed to do now?

6) Use speech which includes an accent or slang.
For example: "Whatcha gonna do wiv that?" Mark grumbled.

7) Try broken speech.
Try to miss out parts of the speech to show the character's feelings.
For example: "I'm sc…sc…scared!" Lucy stammered.

8) Try changing the tense and/or voice.
Try changing one sentence or section from the past to the present tense, to make it sound more real and urgent. You could also try changing from the 3rd person to the 1st person to help the reader identify more closely with how the character is feeling.
For example: He stared ahead looking at the entrance to the woods. It's just a cluster of trees, he told himself. No reason to be afraid. Walk forward. But somehow he could not slow down his racing heart.

DEVELOPING SKILLS

Punctuation

It is obviously important in all pieces of writing that **punctuation** is used correctly throughout. However, to really push your story ahead of the pack, you need to try and use a range of punctuation. Here is some ambitious punctuation that you can try and include in your stories to make them top notch!

Speech marks "…"

- **Speech always starts with a capital letter, unless it is an interrupted sentence.**

    For example: He asked, "Have you any cornflakes?"

    For example: "They are not," she said, "going to see the film."

- **There must always be a piece of punctuation before the last speech mark. This can be a comma, exclamation mark or a question mark if the sentence is continuing. If the sentence is ending, it needs to be a full stop.**

    For example: "Have you anything to say to me?" he demanded.
    "No, I'm afraid I haven't."

- **Whenever a new person speaks, it must start on a new line.**

    For example: Amir asked, "What is the matter?"
    "I don't know," she replied.

Brackets (…) and Dashes -

- **Brackets and dashes can be used to add more detail to a sentence. The sentence must make sense without the brackets/dashes. Both are slightly informal.**

    For example: The girl (who always had a smile) greeted the parents enthusiastically.

    For example: The girl - who always had a smile - greeted the parents enthusiastically.

DEVELOPING SKILLS

Semi-colon ;

- **Semi-colons are used to link sentences that are closely related. Both sentences must be main clauses.**

  For example: The forest was silent and absolutely still; Flora was excited to venture inside and explore.

Colon :

- **Colons can be used to expand a sentence. The second part is often an explanation or continuation of an idea previously presented. It is more formal than a dash.**

  For example: There was only one thing that she wanted to do: dive into the crystal-clear ocean.

See if you can re-write this paragraph adding punctuation and capital letters.

> we are not nicola demanded going home without dipping our toes into the sea nicola who was always adventurous was desperate to dive into the sea with her sister but I'm too scared dani yelled grabbing dani's hand nicola dragged the two of them forward running across the golden sand and towards the ocean the gentle waves lapped against the shore the sun glistening on the sparkling water there was only one thing left to do it was time to dive.

Write here:

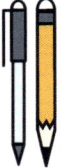

DEVELOPING SKILLS

Writing Tasks

To conclude the chapters, it is time for you to practise using your knowledge of language and skills to write some short pieces of creative writing. Read the model example below.
Can you spot different language techniques and skills?

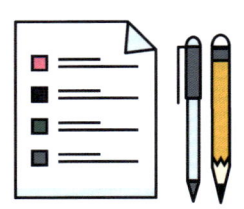

Model example:

Priya woke with a jump. It was 7am on July 22nd and it was her birthday. She looked out the window and saw that the sky was a shimmering, dazzling blue. Clouds, like fluffy cotton balls, drifted across the sky. Priya had been waiting for her birthday for too long. All her friends had already turned 10 years old and finally it was her turn. She brushed her unruly, black hair and pulled on her favourite chequered dungarees, before heading downstairs.

Gobbling her breakfast, Priya was desperate to visit their neighbour. Her mum had told her that her birthday present was waiting there for her. Priya's heart started to race like a train pounding down the tracks, as she wondered what her present could be. Last year, her parents had bought her new clothes and some hideous shiny shoes. Priya was not the type of girl who cared about her appearance and so she found it hard to conceal her disappointment. This year, she desperately hoped for something different. Something better.

Excitedly, she ran outside and knocked on the door. The sun's merciless heat beat down on her as she waited impatiently on the doorstep.
No answer. Knock, knock. Suddenly, the large, wooden door creaked open and her neighbour's son, Tyler, was standing there, with a wide grin and large eyes that sparkled like diamonds. Knowing that he already knew what her present was, Priya pushed forward and sprinted down the corridor into their living room.

In the middle of the floor, she gasped at the large box. Although it was wrapped up in purple and gold paper, there were holes dotted all over it. Before she had the chance to rip open the paper, she heard the most wonderful noise. Woof! Woof!

General Checklist

- [ ] Could you describe the **time of day** and perhaps the **season**?
- [ ] Could you describe the **weather**, perhaps using **personification**?
- [ ] Could you describe something with a **simile** or a **metaphor**?
- [ ] Could you change your **sentence starter**, by adding in an adverb/-ed/-ing word (**ISPACED**).
- [ ] How is your character **feeling**? Could you use **Show Don't Tell**?
- [ ] Could you describe your **character** by using some **ambitious adjectives**?
- [ ] Could you describe the **setting**? Use your **senses**.
- [ ] **What happens next?** Move the story on!

DEVELOPING SKILLS

Writing Task 1:

We have given you the basic storyline, highlighted in bold. Your job is to pad out the story with fabulous language and skills, using the checklist on the side of the page to support you.
Good luck!

Story: "Lost"

Alex sprinted through the field and towards the woods, hoping that the man chasing him had given up and left him alone.

After entering the woods, he soon found shelter and stopped to catch his breath.

Panicking, Alex looked around and realised that he was lost.

All of a sudden, he noticed a torchlight beaming against his clothes.

© 2019 Bright Light Education Ltd · Creative Writing Skills · 43

DEVELOPING SKILLS

Writing Task 2:

This time, you choose where to add in the sentences below:
- Jesse and his mum left the house and headed to the shops.
- Unexpectedly, he saw an unusual shop ahead of him, which he had never seen before.
- Suddenly, he gasped as he looked to the very corner of the shop.

Story: "The Shop"

"Do I have to go shopping with you, mum? It's so boring," Jesse grumbled.

✓ General Checklist

- ☐ Could you describe the **time of day** and perhaps the **season**?
- ☐ Could you describe the **weather**, perhaps using **personification**?
- ☐ Could you describe something with a **simile** or a **metaphor**?
- ☐ Could you change your **sentence starter**, by adding in an adverb/-ed/-ing word (**ISPACED**).
- ☐ How is your character **feeling**? Could you use **Show Don't Tell**?
- ☐ Could you describe your **character** by using some **ambitious adjectives**?
- ☐ Could you describe the **setting**? Use your **senses**.
- ☐ **What happens next?** Move the story on!

Writing Task 3:

This time, can you write the short story, based on this simple story plan?
- **Start:** Your character gets in the car to be driven to stay with her aunt for the summer holidays, because her parents have to work.
- **Middle/Problem:** Your character arrives, and the most unusual lady opens the door to the house. Something funny happens.
- **End:** Your character goes to her bedroom and unpacks. She decides that it might be a fun summer holiday after all.

Story: "Summer Holidays"

Hints: Time of day, weather, how is your character feeling, who is your character, have they met the aunt before? What's the journey like?

Hints: Describe the aunt and the house. Describe one small fun incident (something at dinner time?)

DEVELOPING SKILLS

Creative Writing Skills

DEVELOPING SKILLS

Writing Task 4:

The next challenge is to see whether you can write a suspense paragraph. This time, you are not writing a full story, but instead a descriptive paragraph full of suspense. The aim is for you to keep your reader on edge for as long as possible, without including too many dramatic events. The fear needs to be in the reader's imagination!

Story: " _____ " (Enter your title)

Finn woke up with a jump. He heard a faint thud from the kitchen downstairs...

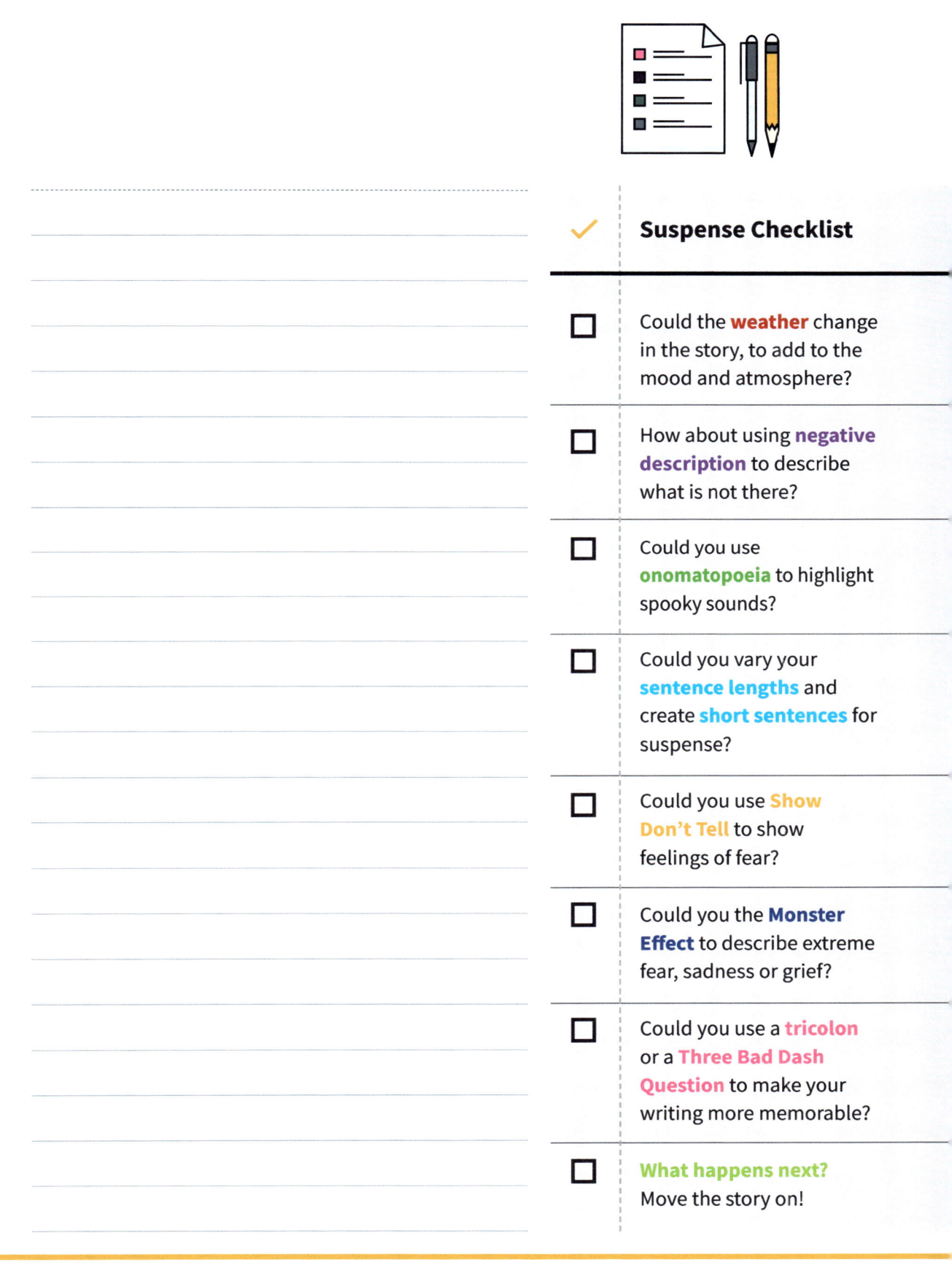

DEVELOPING SKILLS

✓	**Suspense Checklist**
☐	Could the **weather** change in the story, to add to the mood and atmosphere?
☐	How about using **negative description** to describe what is not there?
☐	Could you use **onomatopoeia** to highlight spooky sounds?
☐	Could you vary your **sentence lengths** and create **short sentences** for suspense?
☐	Could you use **Show Don't Tell** to show feelings of fear?
☐	Could you the **Monster Effect** to describe extreme fear, sadness or grief?
☐	Could you use a **tricolon** or a **Three Bad Dash Question** to make your writing more memorable?
☐	**What happens next?** Move the story on!

DEVELOPING STRUCTURE

Now, it's time to learn how to structure your story.

Creating a Plan

Now you have learned about language and skills, it is time to learn about developing structure whilst having a go at writing your first full short story. It can really help to make a quick **plan** of what you are going to write about. There are many ways to plan a story so choose the method that you find works well. On the following page is a simple plan which you may like to use.

Remember that your story must include:

1 START
Who are your characters?
Where will it take place?

2 MIDDLE
What will happen in the story?
What is the problem?

3 END
How will the problem be resolved?
How will it end?

Task:

Use one of the following story ideas to plan your story on the following page. If you prefer to use your own story idea, feel free!

- The Fire
- It was the wrong pet!
- A new discovery!

DEVELOPING STRUCTURE

Title: _____

HOW WILL IT START?

_____
_____
_____
_____
_____
_____

WHAT WILL HAPPEN?

_____
_____
_____
_____
_____
_____

HOW WILL IT END?

_____
_____
_____
_____
_____
_____

CHARACTERS:

- _____
- _____
- _____
- _____
- _____
- _____

SETTING:

- _____
- _____
- _____
- _____
- _____
- _____

DEVELOPING STRUCTURE

Describing the Character

Now you have made a rough plan, it's time to **start** your story.
A straightforward way to begin is to describe your **main character**.
When describing your character, consider the following:

1) What does your character's **face** look like?
For example: Her sharp angular cheekbones jutted out of her face like a shark's fin.

2) What **clothes** is your character wearing?
For example: He wore shapeless, oversized clothes which were usually creased and full of holes.

3) What **sounds** does your character make?
For example: She spoke always with a high-pitched chirp and seemed excited even in the most boring situations.

4) What does your character **smell** like?
For example: Every time he spoke, the stench of rotting cabbage filled the room.

5) What is your character's **personality** like?
For example: She was as bubbly as a glass of champagne.

6) Does your character have any weird and wonderful **hobbies or habits**?
For example: He always gives the most grotesque snort at the end of a laugh, oblivious to the disturbed reaction of those around him.

TOP TIP!

Try not to say the usual boring aspects of the character, such as, 'He has blue eyes'. Write something more unique and unusual! Think about things like jewellery, scars and wounds, bruises, painted nails, moles and freckles, the shape of a character – the list is endless!

For example:
Milo hated being Milo. He hated the way his wiry hairs poked out of his nostrils.
He despised how he was shorter than everyone in the class - and the class below. Last of all, he resented his mother for making him wear an oversized school uniform to save on money.

DEVELOPING STRUCTURE

Have a look at the image of the person below. **Annotate** the image with some ideas for describing his features.

Face:

Smells:

Clothes:

Personality:

Sounds:

Hobbies:

TOP TIP!

When you write about your character, rather than writing about all their features, it can sometimes be more effective to focus on just one of their most interesting features.

For example: (Here we've focused on the character's eyes)

Khalid's narrow flint eyes were set deeply into the folds of his skin. He glared ahead, unblinking as if he was in a trance. Quietly, he observed every detail and every move.

Now your turn!
Choose another feature from the image above and write a few sentences to describe him!

DEVELOPING STRUCTURE

Describing the Setting

Not only is it important to have a strong, visual character, but you also want your reader to be able to picture in their minds where your story is taking place. You could also start your story by describing the **setting**:

1) What is the **weather** like?

For example: The first rays of sunshine leapt from the sky to light up the sleeping homes.
For example: The clouds wept incessantly until every road was flooded.

2) How would you describe the **buildings** or **town**?

For example: It was a picturesque town with quaint alleyways and leafy gardens.
For example: The crumbling Georgian house sat alone at the end of the dark street.

3) How would you describe the **nature**?

For example: A towering forest lived at the end of his garden.

4) What can be **heard**?

For example: The town was always eerily silent. No birds would sing and it was as if the town was holding its breath waiting for something to happen.

5) What can be **smelled**?

For example: Whenever she stepped outside, she was overcome by the smell of rotting rubbish.

6) How does the scenery make you **feel**?

For example: The dark dampness of the school always left her with a feeling of loneliness and despair.

TOP TIP!

Try not to say the usual boring aspects of the setting, such as, 'It was a hot, sunny day'. Write something more creative!

For example:

David lived with his mum on the edge of town on the top floor of a high-rise building. You might think that this would offer beautiful views of the surrounding snow-capped mountains but unfortunately all the windows were cracked and too dirty to see through.

DEVELOPING STRUCTURE

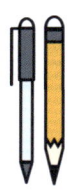

Just like describing your character, you now need to describe the setting. Have a go at annotating the setting below.

Weather:

Buildings:

Nature:

Sounds:

Smells:

Feelings:

TOP TIP!

Similarly, rather than writing about all the features, it can sometimes be more effective to focus on just one of the most interesting features.

For example: (Here we have focused on the trees surrounding the building)

In the distance, the trees were joined together like multi-coloured umbrellas. Patches of sunlight kissed their upper leaves, whilst the smaller more vulnerable trees became shadowed by the towering giants.

Now your turn! Choose another feature from the image above and write a few sentences to describe it!

© 2019 Bright Light Education Ltd   Creative Writing Skills | 53

DEVELOPING STRUCTURE

Describing the Setting – Weather

Describing the **weather** can be an easy way in which to bring some fabulous vocabulary and literary devices into your story. Use these two pages to record some of the phrases that you come across. You never know when you might need them!

SEASONS:

Spring	**Summer**
The grassy verge was alive with vibrant blooms.	*A stifling heat filled the air and sapped their energy.*
Autumn	**Winter**
Like splashes of fire, the leaves scattered the cobbled streets.	*Gnawing away at her fingertips, the icy air continued to drive forward.*

DEVELOPING STRUCTURE

TIME OF DAY:

Early Morning	**Mid Afternoon**	**End of Day**
Beads of dew welcomed the morning sun as it rose above the hills.	*Squinting into the sunlight, there was not a cloud in the sky.*	*Shadows crept closer and closer to the house until, finally, a cloak of darkness surrounded them.*

WEATHER:

Sunny	**Rainy**	**Windy**
The sun's rays poured in through the window and drenched the room.	*She lifted her head to the sky as the heavens opened.*	*The wind tore through the streets.*
Thunder and Lightning	**Snow**	**Mist and fog**
The ominous rumble of thunder could be heard overhead.	*With the never-ending visitors, the pristine powder had turned very rapidly to dirty slush.*	*A veil of fog hung over the village.*

DEVELOPING STRUCTURE

Creating your Character

Using the ideas from the last few pages, can you create your main **character** for your story? Draw your character below and annotate your picture with notes about them!

Can you write one or two sentences to describe one of their features?

Here are a few ambitious adjectives to help you plan who your character will be:
aloof, arrogant, belligerent, clumsy, draconian, flashy, forgetful, frantic, grouchy, malicious, mysterious, secretive, snobbish, thick-skinned, undesirable, voracious.

What name should you give to your character?
Children often find it difficult to come up with an interesting name for their character.
Here are some ways to come up with a good name:

1) If possible, try to create a name which reflects your character's personality! Can you think of any famous characters from books who have an interesting name? Jot three names down here:

2) You could also try using alliteration. Can you come up with two more names using alliteration?

   Buzz the Bee-Keeper

   What will the name of your character be?

56 | Creative Writing Skills © 2019 Bright Light Education Ltd

DEVELOPING STRUCTURE

Creating your Setting

The next task is to think about describing your **setting**.
Draw your setting below and annotate your picture with notes about it!

Can you write one or two sentences to describe your setting?

What name should you give to the street, the town or the building?
Children often find it difficult to come up with an interesting name for their setting.

Here are some ways to come up with a good name:

1) If possible, try to create a name which reflects the mood of the story. Can you think of any famous streets, towns or buildings from books which have an interesting name?

   Jot three streets, towns or buildings down here:

   _____   _____   _____

2) You could also try using alliteration. Can you come up with two more street names, towns or buildings using alliteration?

   Sunnyhill Street
   _____

   What will the name of your setting be? _____

© 2019 Bright Light Education Ltd | Creative Writing Skills | 57

DEVELOPING STRUCTURE

Story Starter

When you start your story, you want to grab the reader's attention in your first few sentences. We call this the 'Story Starter'. This might be a powerful description of the main character or setting, but there are other ways in which you could start:

---

1) Start with **dialogue** or a **sound effect.**

For example: "Do I have to go to Saturday school, mum?" Enzo grumbled whilst reluctantly putting on his shoes.

2) Start with a **dramatic** event.

For example: Layla sprinted across the lawn, her heart thumping and her sweaty hand clasping the bronze key that would turn her summer holidays upside down.

3) Start with a **question**.

For example: Have you ever seen your life flash before your eyes? I have.

4) Start with a sequence of **short sentences** contrasting with a longer sentence.

For example: Thunder. A single crack of thunder. Gemma looked up to the cloudless sky and wondered how a beautiful blue panorama could produce such a terrifying sound.

5) Start by describing the **time** or the **weather.**

For example: The clock struck midnight and he realised that the most important day of his life so far had just begun.

6) Start with a **flashback.**

For example: As I wandered along the lonely cliff path, my mind took me back to twenty years ago and that terrible stormy night when my life changed forever.

DEVELOPING STRUCTURE

TASK:
Using your story idea, write three different versions for the start of the story.
Which one did you like best?

Version 1:

Version 2:

Version 3:

STORY STARTER TOP TIPS:
- **Choose one of the options listed to start your first sentence.**
- **Look at how other novels start their stories.**

DEVELOPING STRUCTURE

First Paragraph

You have now chosen a great **story starter** which grabs the readers' attention in the first few seconds. Now you have to write your **first paragraph(s).**

Remember for the first paragraph(s) you need to include the following:
- **Character description.**
- **Setting description.**
- **Some action.**
- **Don't forget language and skills too!**

EXAMPLES

Here are two examples of a story starter together with the first paragraph(s). You will notice the story starter can be very separate to the first paragraph(s) as seen in Example 1, or it can follow on from the story starter as seen in Example 2.

Example 1:

Layla sprinted across the lawn, her heart thumping and her sweaty hand clasping the bronze key that would turn her summer holidays upside down.

It had started as another monotonous day at her aunt's house. Layla had moaned to her mother about having to spend her holidays there with no one to play with, the same old boring toys and being miles from any village. "I've got to work," came her mother's reply. It wasn't as if her aunt's house was particularly grand - it was, in fact, creaky and ill-kept, and Layla had once got a splinter by running her hand up the banister - but it was large: much bigger than her own. However big it was though, it lacked any excitement and Layla yearned for something exciting in her life, especially to wile away her summer holidays.

Example 2:

Thunder. A single crack of thunder. Gemma looked up to the cloudless sky and wondered how a beautiful blue panorama could produce such a terrifying sound.

Gemma had started to wonder whether it was actually thunder she had heard at all. The sun had been shining ahead of her but, looking in her rear-view mirror, the ominous clouds were creeping up on her. She put her foot to the accelerator and pressed hard. There was only an hour until sunset and she still had at least 70 miles to cover before she reached her destination. Her already frayed nerves were made worse by the fact she didn't know the road and had no sat-nav to guide her. She was petrified of the thought of driving on these windy, un-tarmacked and unfamiliar roads in the dark and in the midst of a thunderstorm. She kept asking herself over and over again, "Why, oh why did I agree to do this?" But there was no use questioning the decision now. She was beyond the point of no return. There was simply no turning back.

DEVELOPING STRUCTURE

You are now ready to write that **first paragraph!** Don't forget to use the checklist below, to ensure that you've made it as captivating as possible!

Write here:

First Paragraph Checklist:

- ✓ Did you describe your main character?
- ✓ Did you set the scene?
- ✓ Did you include some action?
- ✓ Have you included language and skills throughout?

DEVELOPING STRUCTURE

Developing the Main Story

It's now time to think about the **main, middle** part of your storyline. Refer to your plan. There is usually some kind of problem that needs to be overcome on one particular day. Remember, at this stage, you are only writing a short story so try to limit yourself to one main event!

For example:

An unexpected event?

An accident?

Something gets lost?

A vehicle breaks down?

Something is stolen?

With the middle of the story you need to:

- Continue the storyline from the first paragraph(s).

- Build up to your main event or problem in the story. Using short sentences contrasted by long sentences can help to build this suspense. Rhetorical questions are also good at building up to the climax.

- Ensure you continue to add character and setting descriptions throughout.

- Include your language and skills too!

DEVELOPING STRUCTURE

TOP TIP!

Keep your storyline straightforward and convincing. Stay in the same tense, usually the past tense is the easiest to write in.

Here are some ways in which you might begin the main section:

On one particularly stormy morning, Jasper decided that rather than going to take his dog, Monty, for his usual walk in the local park, instead he would go down the dusty stairs to explore the basement of his house.

OR....

Martha was excited because today was her birthday. As soon as her alarm went off, she jumped out of bed and ran down the stairs. Her face glowed with excitement as she searched for the present that she had been longing for.

EXAMPLES

Below are two examples of story titles, showing how you could start your story and the potential main event or problem. Remember to keep your problem simple!

Example 1:

Title: *The Umbrella*

Story Starter (describing the weather): *A thick blanket of darkness covered the city. Wind blew gusts of car fumes through the streets and it crept under the cracks of doors and whispered down sooty chimneys.*

Possible main event/problem: *The man finds an umbrella which is magical and allows him to fly.*

Example 2:

Title: *Spooked*

Story Starter (starting with dialogue): *"You're not scared are you?" her brother taunted her whilst setting off ahead.*

Possible main event/problem: *Their father asks them to go and visit their grandmother one evening to check on her and her brother suggests they take the short route across the graveyard. As they are walking across, they hear a huge scream.*

DEVELOPING STRUCTURE

Developing the Main Story

TASK:
Use the checklists below to help you to write the middle section of your story on the next page. Remember, you do not have to include every single type of language, skill and technique. You also do not have to follow the order of the checklists. The checklists are to be used as prompts and to support you. **Most importantly, enjoy writing and immerse yourself in the story!**

✓ General Checklist

- ☐ Could you describe the **time of day** and perhaps the **season**?
- ☐ Could you describe the **weather**, perhaps using **personification**?
- ☐ Could you describe something with a **simile** or a **metaphor**?
- ☐ Could you change your **sentence starter**, by adding in an adverb/-ed/-ing word (**ISPACED**).
- ☐ How is your character **feeling**? Could you use **Show Don't Tell**?
- ☐ Could you describe your **character** by using some **ambitious adjectives**?
- ☐ Could you describe the **setting**? Use your **senses**.
- ☐ **What happens next?** Move the story on!

✓ Suspense Checklist

- ☐ Could the **weather** change in the story, to add to the mood and atmosphere?
- ☐ How about using **negative description** to describe what is not there?
- ☐ Could you use **onomatopoeia** to highlight spooky sounds?
- ☐ Could you vary your **sentence lengths** and create **short sentences** for suspense?
- ☐ Could you use **Show Don't Tell** to show feelings of fear?
- ☐ Could you the **Monster Effect** to describe extreme fear, sadness or grief?
- ☐ Could you use a **tricolon** or a **Three Bad Dash Question** to make your writing more memorable?
- ☐ **What happens next?** Move the story on!

DEVELOPING STRUCTURE

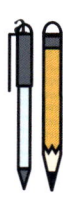

It is now time to write the middle section of your story. Good luck!

Write here:

TOP TIP!

Try to drip feed character and setting details throughout the story.
For example: when your character is speaking, you could say, "Yes," he commented, peering over his thickly rimmed glasses.

DEVELOPING STRUCTURE

Ending the Story

A good ending is important as it forms the final impression left in the reader's mind. Which books have you read which have a memorable ending? Why? Here are some ways in which you might end your story:

---

1) Give your story a **happy** ending.

For example: Ellis crossed the finish line with a huge grin. He had won first prize!

2) Give your story a **sad** or **tragic** ending.

For example: Emily hobbled to the end of the race, with her ankle throbbing.

3) Leave your story on a **cliff-hanger.**

Make sure that the problem has been resolved and you don't just stop mid-way through the story!

For example: The clouds drew in and the eerie sounds of night filled the air. William was alone and terrified.

4) Give your story a **twist** or **surprise ending.**

For example: Unexpectedly, Safa realised that it wasn't a bomb after all. It was a birthday present!

5) Have a **moral** at the end of your story.

For example: Most importantly, Jack learned never to judge a book by its cover.

6) Leave your story with a feeling of **suspense.** Ask a **question!**

For example: Will the spy manage to stop the bomb in time?

7) Have a **circular** ending which takes the reader back to the start, or back to an earlier incident.

For example: Charlotte thought back to how it had all started and wondered whether things might be different had she managed to jump on the train in time.

8) Don't say that it was all a **dream.**

Try to avoid this ending if possible!

DEVELOPING STRUCTURE

TASK:
Just as you did for your story starter, now it is time to think how your story will end.
See if you can jot down ideas for three different story endings. Which one did you like best? It may not be the one that you originally planned!

Version 1:

Version 2:

Version 3:

DEVELOPING STRUCTURE

Ending the Story

It is now time to write the end of your story!

Write here:

TASKS

Story Genres

In this chapter, we look at different writing tasks.

It is good to be aware of the different **story genres** and the features of each genre. What kind of story do you want to write?

GENRE	DEFINITION	FEATURES
Adventure	The characters go somewhere exciting!	-Will there be a fight? -Perhaps they are on a desert island!
Fable	A story that features animals, plants or nature which are given human qualities.	-Moral at the end. *E.g. How the Tortoise won a race.*
Fairy Tale	A story involving fairies and magic.	-Once upon a time… -Love, magic and a happy ending. -Witches and wizards; princes and princesses.
Fantasy	A story not based on reality. Involves imaginary people and places.	-Wizards, mermaids, dragons and fairies. -Magical and enchanted lands. -Special powers.
Flashback	A story that goes back in time to remember a past event.	-You may change the tense from the present to the past.
Horror	A scary story.	-Haunted and old houses. -Surprise and shock.
Mystery (detective)	A story involving a crime that has been committed.	-The main character needs to solve the crime. -Victims, spies and detectives.
Myths and Legends	A story that explains how the world works or how we should treat each other.	-Usually set a long time ago. -Gods and goddesses. -A fantastical beast, a struggle and a hero. *E.g. Theseus and the Minotaur.*
Play	A story that has been written as a play script to be performed.	-Stage directions, character list, setting the scene, no speech marks, scenes.
Poetry	Imaginative language to express ideas. Some poems tell a story; others follow a pattern.	-Rhyme, alliteration, similes, metaphors, personification, etc.
Science Fiction	Stories based on scientific knowledge.	-Often set in the future, involving advanced technology. -Other galaxies, time machines, missions.

TASKS

Write a Story

Now it's time to apply your writing skills and respond to a task. The tasks have been written in the 1st person, but feel free to change them to the 3rd person. Aim to write about a page and a half. Tick when done!

TASK 1

Write a story based on one of the following **ideas.**

STORY IDEAS	✓
You go on a school trip and discover that the school bus has magic powers.	
You wake up to discover that you are on a desert island.	
You have been asked by your mother to look after your younger sibling.	
You are an explorer, but you get lost on one of your trips.	
Imagine that you go into a shop and find something unexpected.	
Write a story in which you are faced with a strange creature staring at you.	
It's the summer holidays and you are sent to stay with your eccentric relative.	
The Fire.	
It was the wrong pet!	
A new discovery.	
Lost!	

Have a go!

TASKS

Continue the Story

TASK 2

Choose one of the examples below. **Continue** the story.

DON'T FORGET:

- **Refer to events and characters.**
- **Make sure your story is in the same tense and person.**
- **Write in the same style as the text.**

    For example: Are there short sentences? If the author uses questions, then add some into yours. If the author uses dialogue, include it in yours.

CONTINUE THE STORY:

1. The sky was a shimmering, dazzling blue. Lizzie looked up to the sky and smiled. She was waiting in anticipation for her guest to arrive, and buzzing with excitement as it was four years since they had last met. The picnic was prepared, and she was filled with smells of delicious strawberries and freshly baked bread. Suddenly, Lizzie heard footsteps. Without a moment of hesitation, she jumped up and looked ahead.

2. I wasn't the type of person to wait around. I lived my life in the fast lane and believed that those who couldn't keep up with me simply missed out. Nevertheless, I was a mostly popular kid and usually did well in my school tests. The boys liked me because of my hair which spiked like a hedgehog; the girls were drawn towards my impish grin. I found school a fun place to be and on the whole kept out of trouble. This day, however, was different. Something out of the ordinary happened at school and it was my job to step in.

Have a go!

TASKS

Write a Description

TASK 3

> Sometimes you simply need to write a description.

POSSIBLE QUESTIONS:

- **Imagine that you are standing on a cliff looking at the sea below you. Describe what you see and how you feel.**

- **Imagine that your train stops in a tunnel in the dark for half an hour. Describe what you see and how you feel.**

DON'T FORGET:

- You are not being asked to write a story - only a description. You do not need to include a full story structure and you do not need much action.

- You may separate your paragraphs with a 'shift' in focus, for example, you may start describing an animal that you spot or a change in weather.

- Fill your description with language and skills. This is the perfect opportunity to fill your writing with imagery, feelings and atmosphere.

  Hint: **Do not worry about making every single sentence descriptive. Too much can make it difficult to read!**

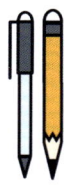

Have a go!

TASKS

Write about an Experience

TASK 4

Sometimes you might be asked to write about an experience.

POSSIBLE QUESTIONS:

- **Write about a time that you or someone else acted courageously. Explain what happened and how you felt.**
- **Write about a time that you or someone else became frustrated by something. Explain what happened and how you felt.**

DON'T FORGET:

- You could respond to the question by writing a story.
- You could also respond to the question by writing a non-fiction recount.
- To show off your creative writing skills most effectively, you might consider writing a fiction story in the third person.
- Don't forget to make the experience the main part of the story!

Have a go!

TASKS

Write about a Picture

TASK 5

Write a story based on the following **image.**

DON'T FORGET:

- **WHAT** is in the picture? (people, landscape…)
- **WHEN** was the picture taken? (time of day…)
- **WHERE** is the picture set? (jungle, forest, countryside, city…)
- **WHY** was this picture chosen? (to give a message, to capture a feeling…)
- **WHO** is in the picture? (people, animals…)
- **HOW** do you feel when you look at the picture? (happy, sad, emotional, excited…)
- Use your senses.
- You should still go through the story writing process, but it must be based on the image.

| Creative Writing Skills | © 2019 Bright Light Education Ltd |

TASKS

Have a go!

ASSESSING MY WORK
Checklist ☑

LANGUAGE:	✓
Have I used some good adjectives, adverbs and verbs?	☐
Have I included ambitious vocabulary?	☐
Have I included figurative language (SHAMPOOP)?	☐
TOTAL:	**/3**

SKILLS:	
Have I used short sentences to create a dramatic effect?	☐
Have I used compound sentences?	☐
Have I used complex sentences?	☐
Have I varied my sentence openers? (ISPACED)	☐
Have I used my senses in my descriptions?	☐
Have I described the feelings of my characters? Have I used Show Don't Tell?	☐
Have I created some suspense?	☐
TOTAL:	**/7**

STRUCTURE, ORGANISATION AND CONTENT	
Have I written in paragraphs?	☐
Have I written in the appropriate form of informal / formal writing?	☐
Have I included appropriate content (based on the task)?	☐
Have I written in the correct genre?	☐
Have I written a good story starter and first paragraph?	☐
Have I written a good middle section?	☐
Have I written a good ending?	☐
Have I shown an understanding of the characters and setting?	☐
Have I included a balance of narrative, description and dialogue?	☐
Have I written with neat handwriting?	☐
TOTAL:	**/10**

SPELLING, PUNCTUATION AND GRAMMAR:	
Have I spelled most words correctly?	☐
Have I punctuated my work correctly?	☐
Have I varied my punctuation? (e.g. exclamation mark, dash, question mark and ellipsis)	☐
Have I written in the correct tense?	☐
Have I ensured that my sentences make sense grammatically?	☐
TOTAL:	**/5**
TOTAL:	**/25**

Self-Assessment

How did you get on? What aspects did you do well? What could you improve upon next time?

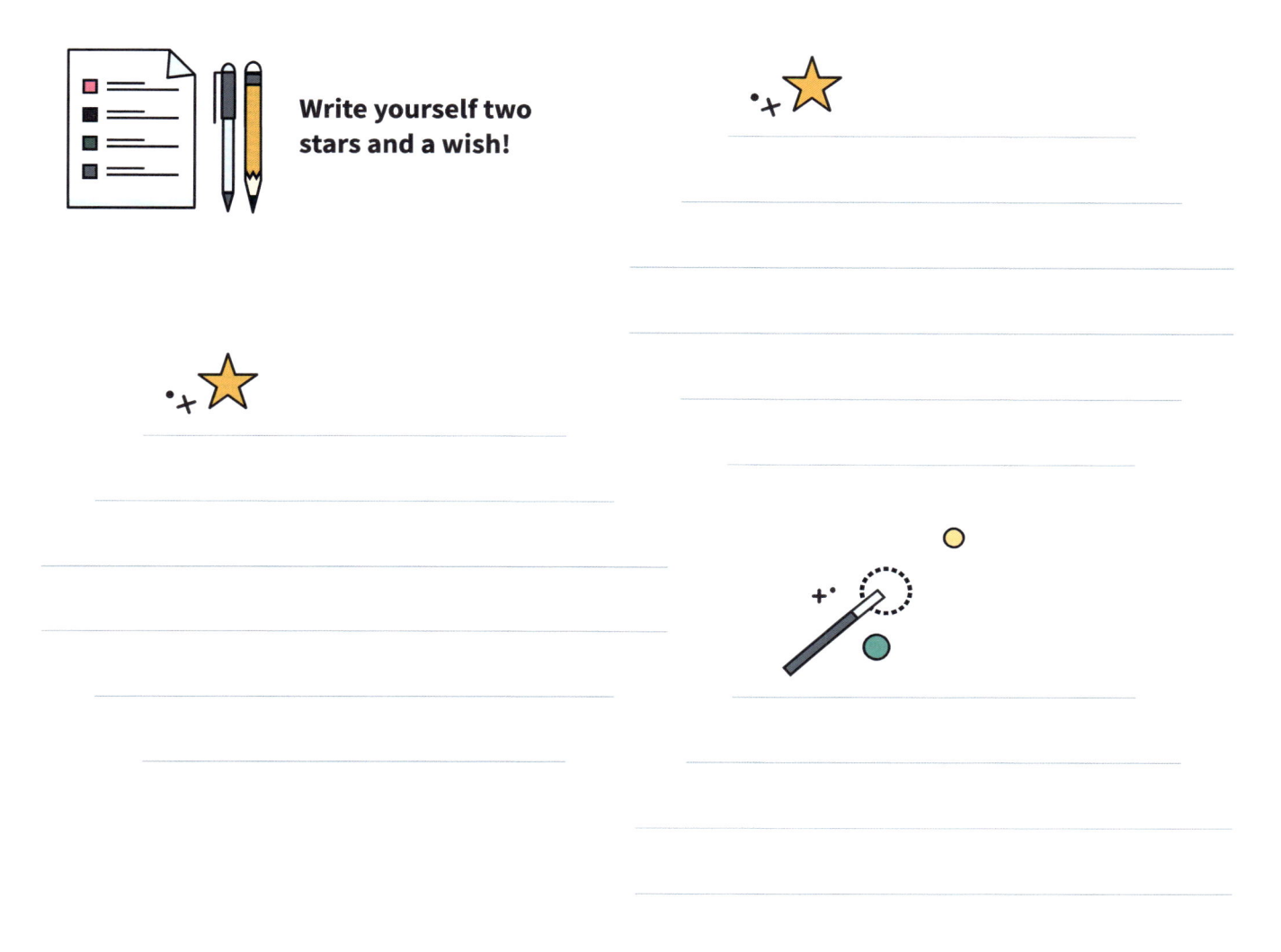

Write yourself two stars and a wish!

CONGRATULATIONS!

You can now write a piece of fiction using **language, skills and structure!**